A Proper Cavalier

The Life and Times of
'Henry'

Henry

Henry's quite the gentleman
With ruffles on his chest,
He doesn't care what day it is
He wears his Sunday best;

Coat of tan and pearly white
Feathered legs and tail,
Eyes as big as chocolate drops –
A most beguiling male.

With velvet nose and silken brow,
Ringlets in his ears,
A real lady-killer now –

A Proper Cavalier!

A PROPER CAVALIER

THE LIFE AND TIMES OF
'HENRY'

BOOK ONE

WRITTEN AND ILLUSTRATED BY
Pauline Sinclair Walden

PUBLISHED BY PHAEDRA

A Proper Cavalier
The Life and Times of Henry

Copyright
Pauline Sinclair Walden 2015

For my husband **Ninian,** who loved spaniels
and
Henry, the little dog who saved my life.

CONTENTS

INTRODUCTION   7

MILLENIUM PUP   8 — 9

BEWARE!   10 - 19

   Cave!

   Macho Male

   Lead on!

   In Your Dreams!

PUPPY LOVE   20 - 33

   Ode to Celia

   Turkish Delight

   Candy

   The Problem with Polly

   Tea Party

   The Rival

SCHOOLDAYS   34 - 41

   Trainer's Delight

   Educating Henry

   Graduation Day

A LEARNING CURVE   42 - 57

   Song of the Flea

   Epicurean Pup

   Frog March

   Paradise lost

   Prelude and Fugue

   The Gull's Way

   Evensong to Nightfall

GOODNIGHT SWEETHEART 58 — 59

INTRODUCTION

Henry was my first dog, and it really was 'love at first sight'; a tiny, four-month-old wriggling bundle of delight who gave me a new sense of purpose after living through the darkest months of my life.

Determined to 'do the right thing' by this new addition to my family of one, I read all the right books and followed their instructions to the letter.

Every day he surprised me with a new antic which I recorded in verse and later illustrated. Advice was heaped upon me in abundance, some heeded, some discarded - hence my proffered warnings to the new dog owner!

While compiling this collection I realised I had far too much content for one volume, hence this is the first of two.

I am sure that my dog-owning readers will identify with these anecdotes and I do hope you will share the joy I have experienced while creating this collection.

Pauline Sinclair Walden

2000!

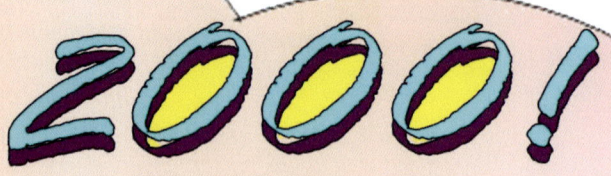

Born when the Millennium
Was only four days old
The cutest of his litter
But the last one to be sold.

His breeder had explained to me,
*'He's not quite - well, you know,
His attributes are not quite those
Required for a show'*.

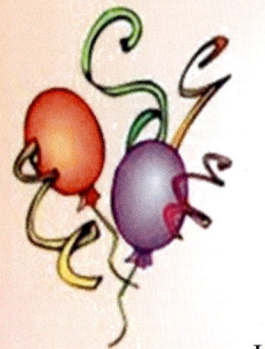

So Henry's not a show dog,
He takes it in his stride;
He knows he's very handsome
But some things he can't hide.

His colouring is perfect
With a lozenge on his head,
Proportions quite impeccable,
Demeanour most well bred.

So there's surely no impediment,
One might very well suppose,
But those endearing imperfections -
The freckles on his nose!

MILLENNIUM PUP

CAVE!
(not *canem* but *opinionem*)
or
BEWARE 'Opinions'!
The Dog's OK!

You must never admit – as I did –
That this is your first canine friend,
To do so invites
Gratuitous advice
Of which, you'll find out, there's no end.

You'll be told about feeding – as I was –
Each one's favourite brand name divulged;
'Only one meal a day',
That's what most of them say,
'And never a fancy indulge!'

When he pulls on his lead – as mine does –
And happily jumps up and down,
'You must train him to do
'What you want him to',
Never mind he's a will of his own!

When he squats on the pavement – as mine did –
A voice close behind loudly booms
'You must know it's better
'To poop in the gutter!'
Who may I ask's kidding whom!?

Of course, I'm not saying it isn't well meant
And is certainly not wholly bad,
But too much can confuse
Till you finally lose
Any confidence you may have had.

So when you've had enough – as I have –
As you fondle your sleek, healthy pup,
Shall I tell you what I say?
No, you'll work out your own way
Of finally shutting them up!

Macho Male

"Aren't you going to have him *'done'?'*
What! and spoil my Henry's fun?
Albeit regulated,
To those who would be mated –
By their owners, I must add,
Lest you all go raving mad
And hurl the accusation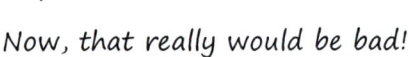
That I am the causation
Of gross proliferation!
Now, that really would be bad!

**(That they should be so lucky
To have my Henry's puppies!)**

Lead On!

'You should let him off his lead!'
Never mind he may not heed
When you call - then hold your breath
As you're frightened half to death
While he legs it out of sight.

You foresee a sleepless night
Of wandering the streets,
The dark and lonely beach,
All the gulls asleep -
And you vow you'll never,
Ever, let him off his leash!

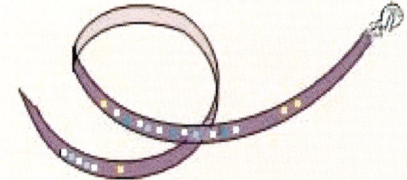

In Your Dreams Henry!

'Don't put him out to stud!
You'll lose him in a flood
Of wild anticipation
For his next gratification -
And that'll do no good!'

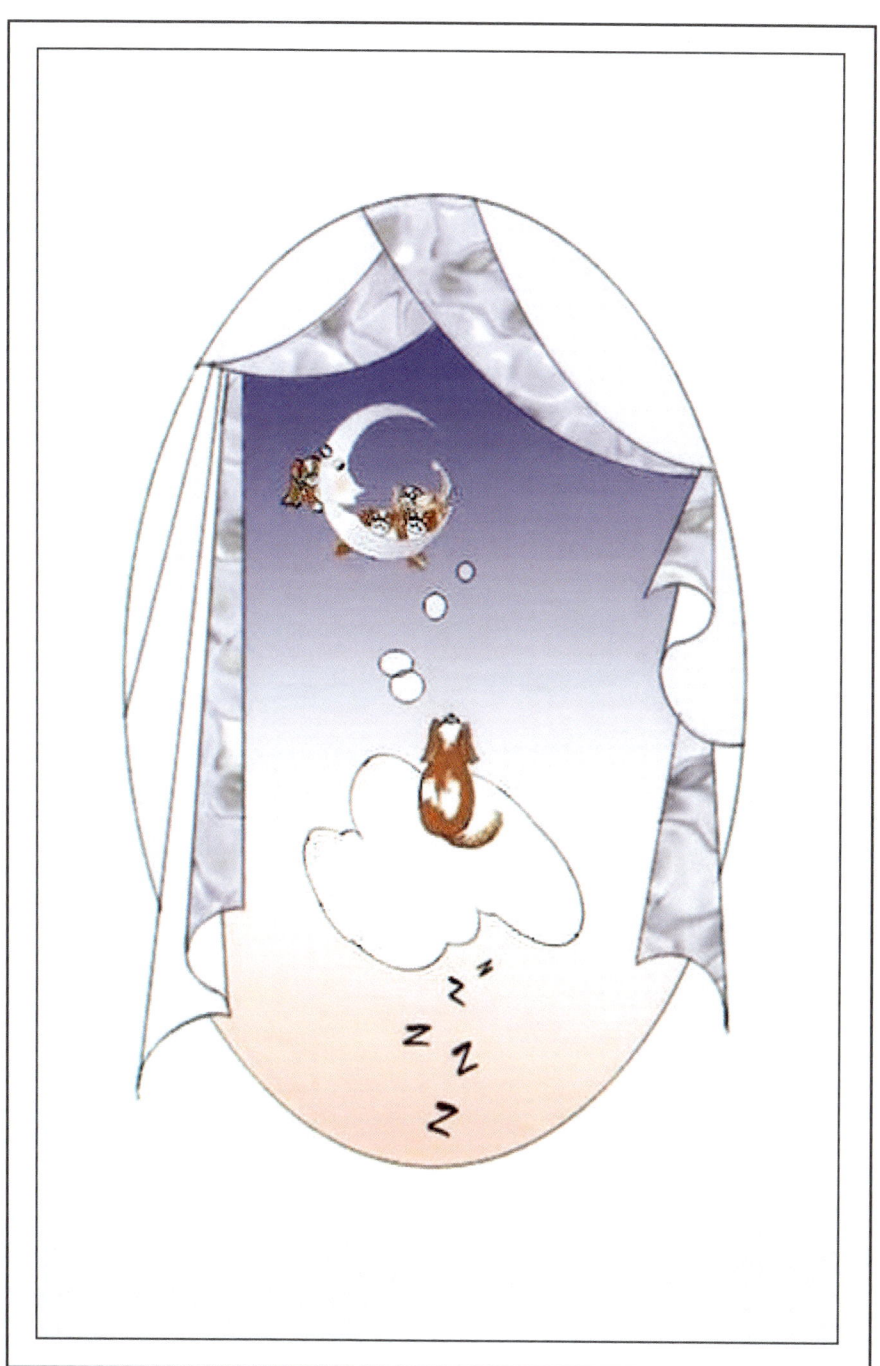

Ode to Celia

Celia, Oh! Celia
Love of my life,
When I grow up
I shall make you my wife.

Although I'm perplexed
That your claws are so long,
Your ears are so pointed,
Your voice is so strong;

When I approached you
You scratched me and spat,
I heard Mistress say
It's because you're a cat.

I know Mistress loves me,
My welfare at heart,
But why so determined
To keep us apart?

Celia, Oh! Celia,
Forever I'll pine,
My love for you thwarted,
You'll never be mine!

Turkish Delight

Henrys heart has mended
Since Celia's show of spite,
But he's fallen, yet again,
For another cat who's white!

A very splendid Lady,
Of Turkish origin
With rather grand demeanour
And a dimple in her chin.

Henry's fascination
For Sully's regal grace
Is apparent from the look
Of adoration on his face.

His approach is far more cautious
Than it was to his first love;
Perhaps he's learned his lesson
From Celia's rebuff.

And yet I fear this new romance
Will suffer the same fate,
As Henry's yet to realise

That cat and dog can't mate!

Henry's not discerning
When looking for romance,
Dog, cat, male or female,
It's all a game of chance.

I foresee a future
Of skirmishes galore -
But he'll soon get his come-uppance
With the boxer bitch next door!

Her mistress calls her 'Candy',
Which belies her fearsome stance,
Henry watches through the fence
With his best 'come hither' glance.

Her answer is a rumbling growl
Which Henry doesn't heed,
But Candy is no lady
And very big indeed!

The Problem with Polly

Polly is a big black bitch
   Of friendly disposition,
Somewhat doubtful parentage
And little inhibition.

But Henry loves her dearly,
A reciprocal affair,
Though, sadly, she's unable
To provide him with an heir.

She's had the 'operation',
But Henry's unaware
As she flirts with him outrageously
And doesn't seem to care

   If Henry's hopes are cruelly dashed
   When doggie intuition
   Persuades him that his fondest dream
   Can never reach fruition.

Perhaps he'll bow out gracefully,
Although it seems ironic
To realise his first true love
Can only be platonic!

Tea Party!

When Henry was invited
To Polly's house for tea,
No-one thought that he would take
The opportunity to pee
On Polly's freshly laundered bed,
A soft and downy pillow,
Of colour somewhat nondescript,

But now bright primrose
yellow!

Polly has a Rival!!

'Ethel' is her name,
With all her bits and pieces
And clearly on the game.

She's a great big Irish Wolfhound
Of fearsome countenance -
Not apparent when engaging
In her ritual courtship dance

Which mystifies poor Henry,
Novice that he is,
Who isn't sure which end is which
Nor which is hers or his!

Ethel's tall and, as they say,
With legs up to her bottom,
A feature of the breed, and she
Was carefully begotten.

Henry, less than half her size,
In fear and trepidation
Standing nimbly on his toes
Attempts investigation.

He's quickly disenchanted
With this hazardous pursuit
As Ethel promptly flattens him
With one enormous foot.

Nothing daunted, he approaches
By a slightly different tack -
A flying leap which, sadly,
Only lands him on his back.

He pauses to renew his strength
For one last desperate bound,
But Ethel's insurmountable -

He's too close to the ground!

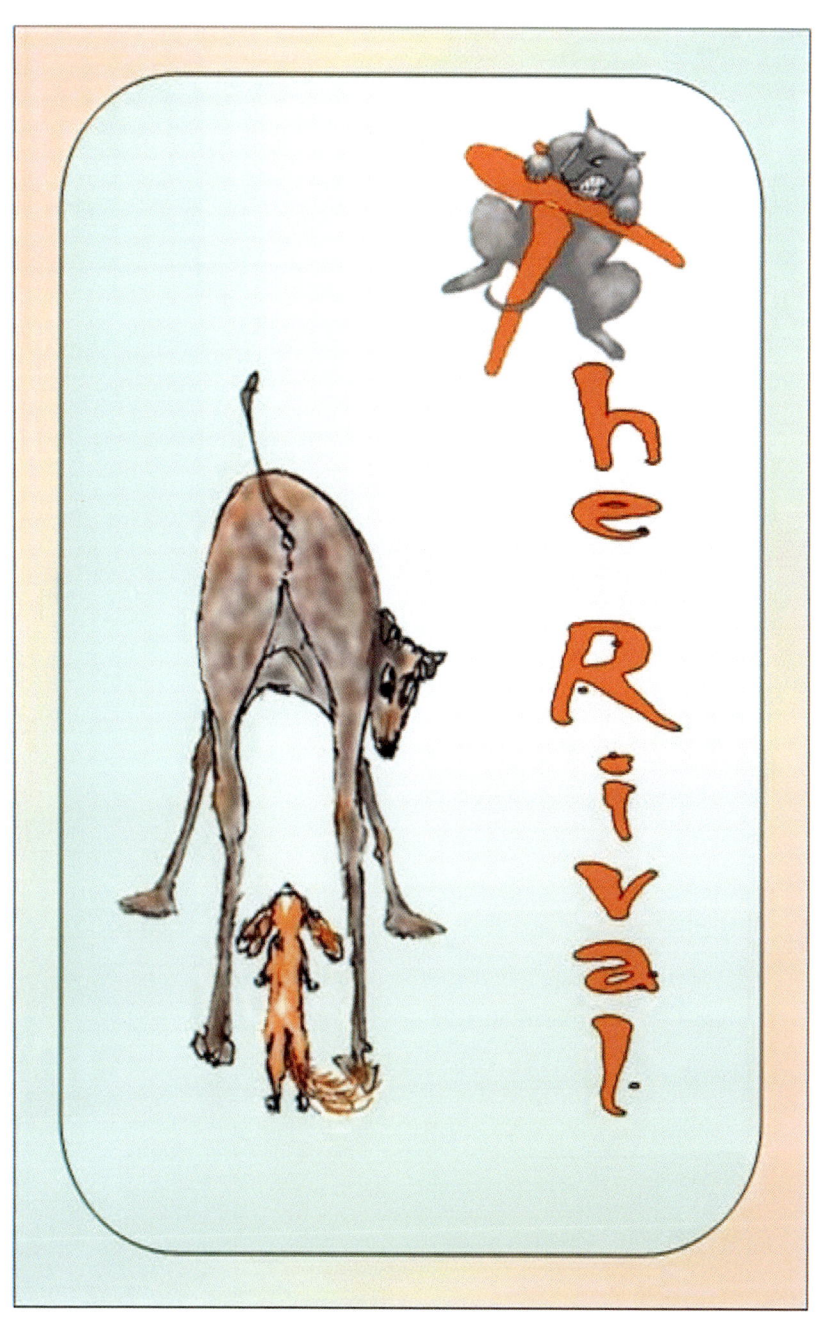

Trainer's Delight

There he goes, on his toes,
I wonder if his trainer knows?
You bet he does! With voice of steel
He promptly calls him back to heel,

Then smugly smirks, *'That's how it's done'*,
But Henry's having too much fun;
He's spied a friend across the green
And soon he's nowhere to be seen!

His trainer legs it in pursuit
But Henry's far too fleet of foot;
My turn to smirk, that *'know-it-all'*,

Pride often comes before a fall!

Educating Henry

They're not agog with bated breath
   In keen anticipation
As would befit all youthful pups
Preparing for instruction.

Instead there's pandemonium,
More like a rugger scrum,
With wagging tail and sniffing nose
Each up another's bum!

When the trainer makes her entrance
The boisterous mood subsides;
On leads grasped firmly once again
Their owners close beside.

Now Henry, always biddable
When told to 'sit' and 'stay',
Seems to misinterpret
And refuses to obey -

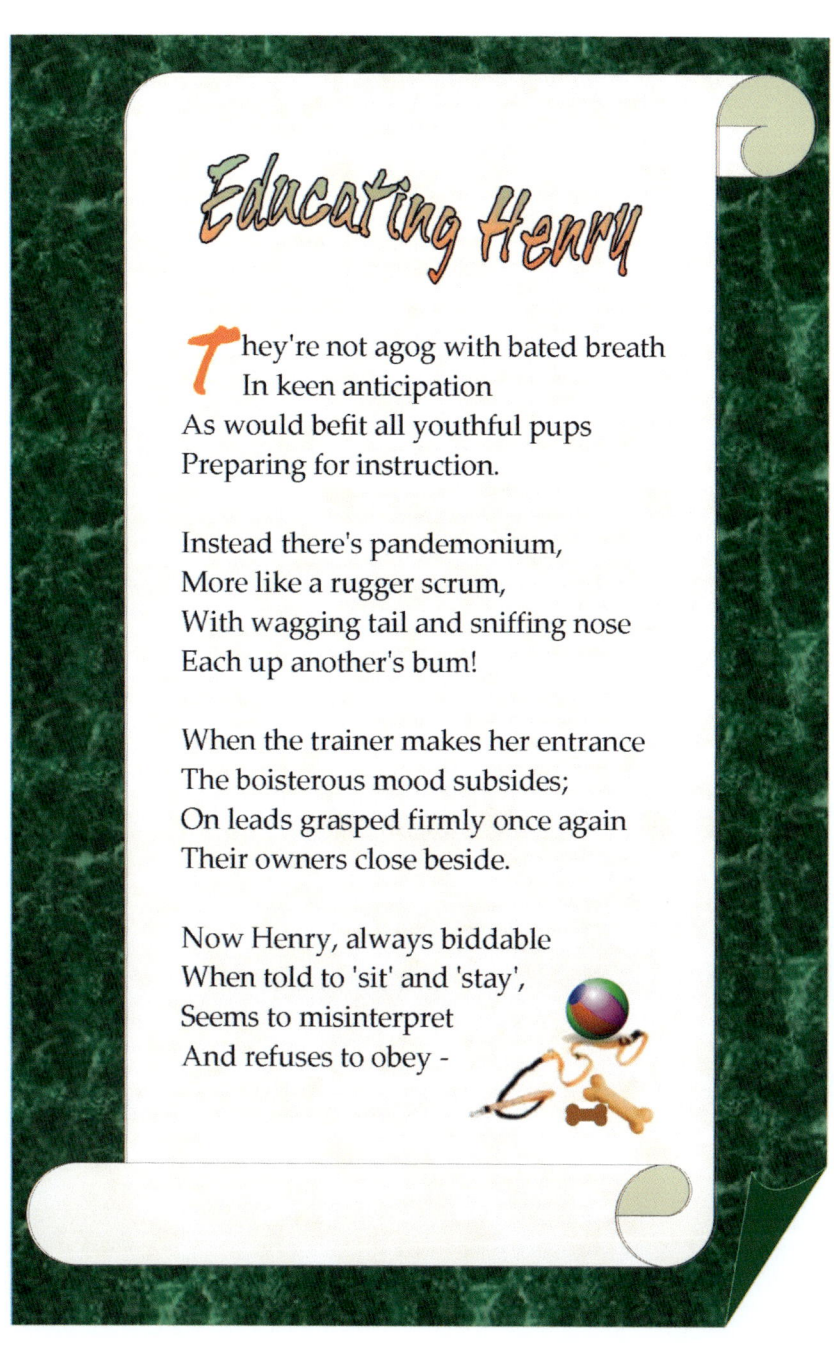

When the trainer gives the same command
  He yips with wicked glee
    And promptly drops a package
    Intending all to see

How clever, how obedient
  He is - how can it be?
    It seems he's got it wrong again
    And scurries back to me.

The next command, to 'fetch' and 'come',
  Suffers a different fate,
    He fetches other puppies treats
    And gobbles them in haste

Lest Mistress take them from him,
  Although she should have known
    That other puppies' treats
    Are always tastier than
    one's own!

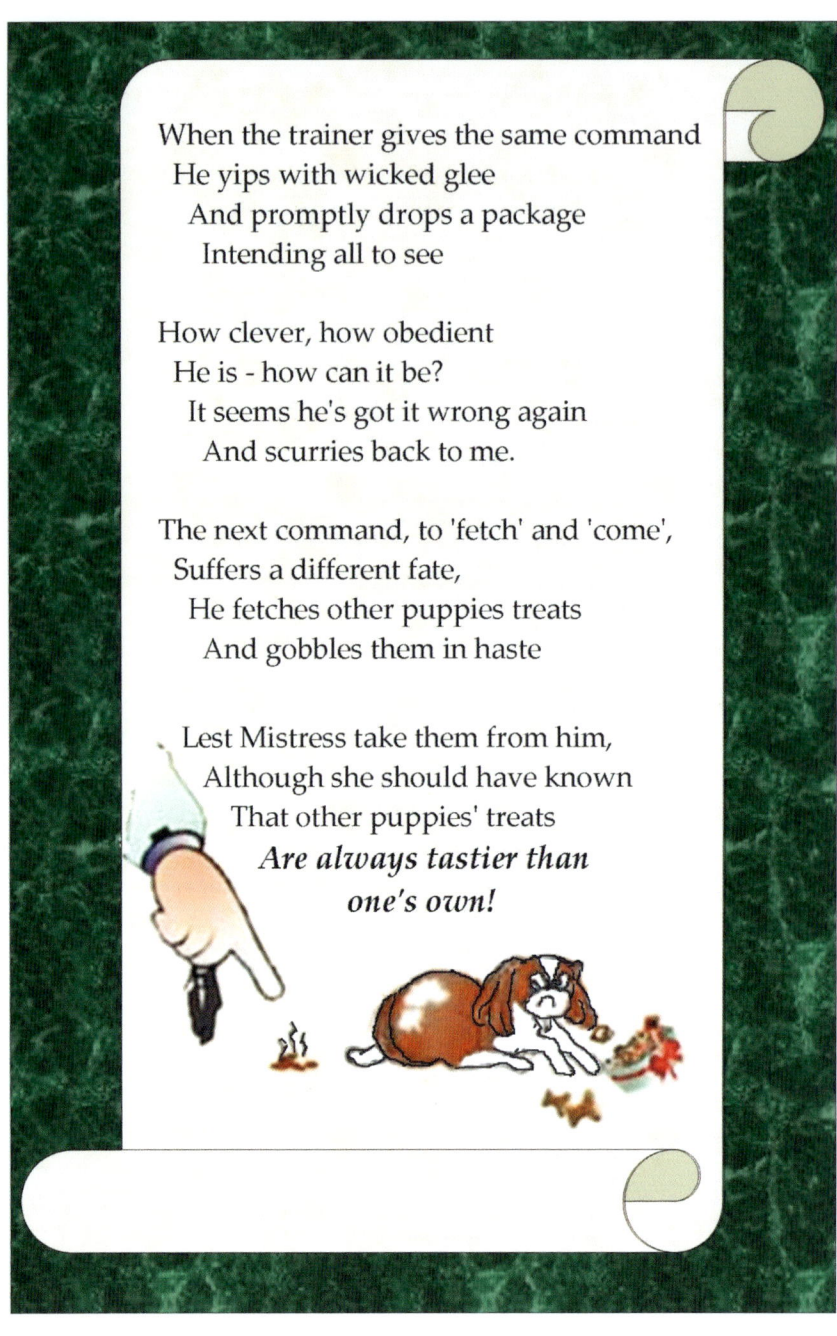

Graduation Day!

Henry's graduated,
Believe it if you can!
Not quite with first class honours,
More of an *'also-ran'*.

Song of the Flea

Oh! Woe is me to be a flea
That cannot reproduce;
That awful stuff they fed my host
Has put me out of use.

Oh! Woe is me to be a flea,
Although things could be worse;
The other stuff they haven't tried
Would put me in a hearse!

(It did!)

Epicurean Pup

Henry, like all spaniels,
Affects a soulful air,
Especially when the menu
Excludes his favourite fare.

He approaches it with caution
As if it's going to bite,
With outstretched neck he takes a sniff,
Retreats as if in fright.

And oh! that soulful look again,
Those huge imploring eyes!
But Mistress is implacable
He's yet to realise;

If he doesn't eat it now
In spite of Mistress' warning,
There's nothing else on offer -

So he'll get it in the morning!

*Dear little Henry,
Darling little dog,
Who'd have thought you capable
Of eating a full grown frog?*

(Nice try, Henry!)

You'd found the stairway to Paradise -
Or so you thought
As you reached the top of the stairs,
(A dog-leg of course)
Before you were caught!

You'd found the stairway to Paradise -
This time you were sure
That no one had seen you,
Or heard your light foot on the stair -

 ON THE
BED!

Prelude and Fugue

The delicate matter of function,
You'll know what I mean I daresay,
Is a source of considerable interest
To one not well versed in the ways

Of dogs' toilet arrangements,
Not discreet like those of the cat,
Who tends to prefer neighbours' gardens –
(Not too sure how I feel about that!)

Now Henry's performance could well be described
Like a prelude and fugue, as in Bach,
I'm sure you'll forgive such a terrible pun but
They're both, after all, merely making their mark!

Henry's prelude consists of a circular dance
Somewhat random one has to concede,
Before finally settling on just the right spot
To comply with his finicky need.

The fugue, well, that settles less quickly
As tune after tune intertwines, like Henry,
Who just when you think that he will
Changes his mind several times.

His finale is rather less thrilling
Than the turbulent end of the fugue,
Although he seems just as unwilling
To finish in one and conclude

What is surely a mere repetition
Of a multiple daily event,
Albeit with some variation –

But For Henry it's effort well spent!

The Gulls' Way

Like a swarm of pterodactyls
   They swoop across the green,
     Dropping tasty morsels
        Which Henry swiftly gleans.

   Their offerings are varied,
     Chicken bones and fishes heads,
  Multi-coloured blobs of gunge.
Soggy bits of bread.

He sniffs the messy packages
With ill-concealed delight,
  As Mistress tries to catch him
    Before he takes a bite!

    He darts among the bushes
      With Mistress in pursuit,
        A chicken bone between his teeth,
         Another favourite food.

         Eventually he's captured
         His struggles all in vain,
         The chicken bone extracted -

        His efforts foiled again!

Goodnight Sweetheart

His little head is drooping
As the gentle arms of sleep
Silently embrace him,
And as he sinks to slumber,
Peace restored once more,
I'm reminded none too gently

That even puppies snore!

Printed in Poland
by Amazon Fulfillment
Poland Sp. z o.o., Wrocław